C000171762

SHROPSHIRE
Wit & Humour

MADELEINE LADD

BRADWELL
BOOKS

Published by Bradwell Books
9 Orgreave Close Sheffield S13 9NP
Email: books@bradwellbooks.co.uk
Compiled by Madeleine Ladd

All rights reserved. No part of this publication may be reproduced, stored in a
retrieval system or transmitted in any form or by any means, electronic,
mechanical, photocopying, recording or otherwise without the prior
permission of Bradwell Books.

British Library Cataloguing in Publication Data: a catalogue record for
this book is available from the British Library.

1st Edition

ISBN: 9781910551073

Print: Gomer Press, Llandysul, Ceredigion SA44 4JL
Design by: jenksdesign@yahoo.co.uk/07506 471162
Illustrations: ©Tim O'Brien 2014

At a primary school in Church Stretton the teacher came up with a good problem for her maths class to solve.

"Suppose, there were a dozen sheep and six of them jumped over a fence," she said to the group of seven-year-olds, "How many would be left?"

Little Harry, a farmer's son, put his hand up. "None," he answered. "None?" exclaimed his teacher. "Harry, I'm afraid you don't know your arithmetic."

"Really, Miss?" said Harry, cockily, "And you dunna know your sheep. When one goes, they all go!"

A gang of robbers broke into the Shrewsbury Lawyers' Club by mistake. The old legal lions put up a fierce fight for their lives and their money. The gang was happy to escape in one piece. "It ain't so bad," one crook said. "At least we got fifty quid between us."

His boss screamed at him, "I warned you to stay clear of lawyers... we had £200 when we broke in!"

Q: What's a Shropshire man's idea of a balanced diet?
A: A pint of scrumpy in each hand

At a cricket match in Alveley a fast bowler sent one down and it just clipped the bail. As nobody yelled "Ow's att", the batsman picked up the bail and replaced it. He looked at the umpire and said, "Windy today, int it?"

"Yes," said the umpire, "Mind it doesn't blow your cap off when you're walking back to the pavilion."

A Shropshire man is driving through Worcestershire, when he passes a farmer standing in the middle of a huge field. He pulls the car over and watches the farmer standing stock-still, doing absolutely nothing. Intrigued, the man walks over to the farmer and asks him, "Excuse me sir, but what are you doing?"

The farmer replies, "I'm trying to win a Nobel Prize."

"How?" Asks the puzzled Shropshire man.

"Well," says the farmer, "I heard they give the prize to people who are outstanding in their field."

The owner of a large company in Shrewsbury went down to check out how everything was going. He notices a young man just relaxing with his feet up in the coffee room. "Just how much are you getting paid a week?" asked the guvnor.

"Two hundred quid!" Replies the young man.

Taking out his wallet, the boss hands him two hundred pounds and says, "Here is a week's pay. Now don't come back!"

A supervisor walks, in with a piece of paper, just as the young man goes out the door. The boss asks him, "How long was that lazy git working here?"

"He doesn't work here," says the supervisor, "He was just waiting for me to give him these directions!"

Many years ago, a miner fell down shaft in the Snail Beach mine.

The deputy shouted, "Have you broken anything, youth?"

"No," called back the miner, "There's not much to break down here!"

Insurance Assessor: "What gear were you in at the moment of the impact?"

Woman Driver: "Gucci sweats and Reeboks."

One day a rich man from Ludlow was driving his Mercedes Benz past a field near Much Wenlock and he saw a shabby man standing there chewing grass. The rich man stopped the car and asked the man, "Why are you eating grass"

The man replied, "I am very, very poor and hungry and I have no money to buy food."

The rich man tells him to climb in the car, "Come home with me to Ludlow."

The poor man shakes his head and says, "But I can't. I have six children out in this field, all eating grass too."

The rich man says, "That doesn't matter, they're all welcome to come home with me to eat."

So the poor man rounds up his kids and they all get in the Mercedes. The poor man can't thank the rich man enough, "I'm so very grateful, sir."

"That's okay," says the rich man, "You should see the grass in my garden, it must be a foot high."

Two aerials meet on a roof, fall in love, get married. The ceremony was rubbish - but the reception was brilliant.

A passenger in a taxi tapped the driver on the shoulder to ask him something.

The driver screamed, lost control of the cab, nearly hit a bus, drove upover the curb and stopped just inches from a large plate glass window.

For a few moments everything was silent in the cab, then the driver said, "Please, don't ever do that again. You scared the daylights out of me."

The passenger, who was also frightened, apologised and said he didn't realise that a tap on the shoulder could frighten him so much, to which the driver replied, "I'm sorry, it's really not your fault at all. Today is my first day driving a cab. I've been driving a hearse for the last twenty-five years."

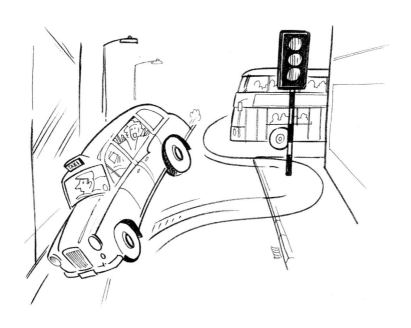

A group of backpackers from Harper Adams University were sitting around a campfire one evening when a stranger asked to join them. Glad to add to their group, they agreed. The evening's fun soon turned to jokes. One of the students started to tell jokes in which Worcester University was the butt of the humour. The stranger who, it turned out, had graduated from Worcester University himself, became more and more furious with each quip. Finally, he had had enough and pulled out his razor and began to threaten the Shropshire lads with it. Fortunately for them, he couldn't find a socket to plug it into.

Why couldn't the lifeguard save the hippie?
He was too far out, man!

Supporters, waiting to watch Telford United play Kidderminster Harriers F.C, heard that the Kidderminster players were going to be delayed.

They saw a sign on the M5 that said "Clean Lavatories"... so they did.

A plain Jane from Wellington goes to see Madame Grizelda, a fortune-teller, and asks about her future love life.

Madame Grizelda tells her, "Two men are madly in love with you – Mark and Maurice."

"Who will be the lucky one?" asks Jane excitedly.

Madame Grizelda answers, "Maurice will marry you, and Mark will be the lucky one."

Telford United beat Kidderminster Harriers five – nothing; they were lucky to get nothing.

"You're looking glum," the captain of Worfield C.C. remarked to one of his players.

"Yes, the doctor says I can't play cricket," said the downcast man.

"Really?" replied the captain, "I didn't know he'd ever seen you play?"

Psychiatrist: "What's your problem?"
Patient: "I think I'm a chicken."
Psychiatrist: "How long has this been going on?"
Patient: "Ever since I was an egg!"

A man from Whitchurch decided to become a monk so he went to the monastery and talked to the head monk. The head monk said, "You must take a vow of silence and can only say two words every three years."

The man agreed and after the first three years, the head monk came to him and said, "What are your two words?"

"Food cold!" the man replied.

Three more years went by and the head monk came to him and said, "What are your two words?"

"Robe dirty!" the man exclaimed.

Three more years went by and the head monk came to him and said, "What are your two words?"

"I quit!" said the man.

"Well," the head monk replied, "I'm not surprised. You've done nothing but complain ever since you got here!"

There's a man in Droitwich who claims to have invented a game that's a bit like cricket; what he doesn't realise is Worcestershire County Cricket Club's been playing it for years.

A Wellington man fell out with his in-laws and banned them from entering the house while he was in it. His wife faithfully carried out his wishes until she was on her deathbed and then asked sadly, "Haven't I always been a supportive wife to you, John?"

"Yes, me duck," he replied, "The best."

"Then I would love it if you could grant my last request and let my sister Sarah ride in the first car with you at my funeral?"

"Alright, me duck," he agreed heavily, "But I'm warning you, it'll spoil all me pleasure!"

Two blokes are standing in the Telford Job Centre, waiting for their turn at the counter.

The first bloke says to the second one, "I have to buy my wife something nice for our wedding anniversary and the benefits cheque won't cover it."

The second bloke looks up from his paper and says, "What date?"

The first bloke thinks for a while and says, "15th September."

The second bloke considers his next question. "What year?"

Without taking a breath, the first bloke replies, "Every year for the last twenty-seven!

Two council workers on a site in Shrewsbury are surveying land they're about to dig up.

The gaffer says to one of them, "You go and get the metal detector and check for pipe work and I'll get the kettle on and have a brew."

The gaffer gets the tea going while his mate starts work. Half-hour later the gaffer puts his paper down, next to his mug of tea, to find out how work is progressing and he finds his mate sitting on a wall scratching his head.

"What's up with you?" The gaffer asks. "There's pipework all over the place. Look!"

The young worker sets off across the land, the bleeper sounding continuously as the detector passes the ground in front of him.

The gaffer watches him, laughing, then he says, "Are you soft or what? You're wearing steel toe caps in your boots!"

Down the King's Head, a group of blokes sit around drinking when a mobile phone on the table rings. One of the men picks up the mobile and puts the speaker-phone on.

A woman's voice says, "How are you, darling? I hope you don't mind but I've just seen a diamond ring priced £2000 and wondered if I can buy it? I've got your credit card with me."

"Of course, my dear, go ahead," answers the man.

"While I'm on," purrs the lady, "I've noticed a top of the range car I'd like. It's only £65,000, could I order that as well?"

"Of course, my angel," replies the man.

His friends around the table look at each other in disbelief as the lady continues, "And I've just noticed a house on the coast, lover. It's only £750,000 - could we have that as well please?"

"Of course, sugar," answers the man, without so much as blinking.

The phone call is ended and the man smiles at the others and takes a long swill of beer. Then he looks around and shouts "Anyone know whose phone this is?"

Q: What do you call a Worcestershire bloke in the 4th Round of the FA Cup?
A: The Referee.

It was match day for Ludlow Town and excited crowds filled the streets, heading for the SBS Stadium. A funeral procession drove slowly through the throng. One of the Ludlow supporters stopped, took off his hat and bowed reverently as the hearse passed.

"That was a nice thing to do," remarked his mate.

"Well," said the Ludlow Town fan, "She was a good wife to me for thirty odd years."

Q: What's the difference between Redditch United and a teabag?

A: A teabag stays in the cup a lot longer.

Two Quatt Cricket Club players are chatting in the bar after a match. "So did you have a hard time explaining last week's game to the wife?" says one.

"I certainly did," says the other, "She found out I wasn't there!"

Derek and Duncan were long-time neighbours in Oswestry. Every time, Derek saw Duncan coming round to his house, his heart sank. This was because he knew that, as always, Duncan would be visiting him in order to borrow something and he was fed up with it.

"I'm not going to let Duncan get away with it this time," he said quietly to his wife, "Watch what I'm about to do."

"Hi there, I wondered if you were thinking about using your hedge trimmer this afternoon?" asked Duncan.

"Oh, I'm very sorry," said Derek, trying to look apologetic, "but I'm actually going to be using it all afternoon."

"In that case," replied Duncan with a big grin, "You won't be using your golf clubs, will you? Mind if I borrow them?"

Three Shropshire women are talking in a bar about a party they've been invited to.

The first one says, "We've got to all wear an item that matches something belonging to our husbands at this party, haven't we?"

"Yeah," said the other two, "But what?"

The first one continued, "Well, my husband's got black hair and I've got a little black dress I can diet into by then."

The second one says, "That's a good idea. My husband has got brown hair and I've got a brown dress I can diet into by then too."

The third one looks a bit hesitant and says, "I just need to go on a diet - my husband's bald!"

"I can't believe it," said the American tourist, looking at the grey skies over the Wrekin, "I've been here an entire week and it's done nothing but rain. When do you guys have summer here?"

"Well, that's hard to say," replied the local. "Last year, it was on a Wednesday."

Darren proudly drove his new convertible into Telford and parked it on the main street. He was on his way to the recycling centre to get rid of an unwanted gift, a foot spa, which he left on the back seat.

He had walked half way down the street when he realised that he had left the top down with the foot spa still in the back.

He ran all the way back to his car, but it was too late...another five foot spas had been dumped in the car.

Ten women out on a hen night in Telford thought it would be sensible if one of them stayed more sober than the other nine and looked after the money to pay for their drinks. After deciding who would hold the money, they all put twenty pounds into the kitty to cover expenses. At closing time after a few spritzers, several vodka and cokes, and a Pina Colada each, they stood around deciding how to divvy up the leftover cash. "How do we stand?" said Sharon.

"Stand?!" said Debbie. "That's the easy part! I'm wondering how I can walk. I've missed the last bus to Shifnal!"

Q: Why was the sheep arrested on the M5?
A: She did a ewe-turn.

A lawyer at Shrewsbury Crown Court says to the judge, "Your Honour, I wish to appeal my client's case on the basis of newly discovered evidence."

His Lordship replies, "And what is the nature of the new evidence?"

The lawyer says, "My Lord, I discovered that my client still has £500 left."

Q: What has eight legs, four ears and twice as much wool as the average sheep?

A: Two sheep.

A man rushed into Royal Shrewsbury Hospital and asked a nurse for a cure for hiccups. Grabbing a cup of water, the nurse quickly splashed it into the man's face.

"What did you that for?" screamed the man, wiping his face.

"Well, you don't have the hiccups now, do you?" said the nurse.

"No," replied the man. "But my wife out in the car does.

A pupil at a school in Oswestry asked his teacher, "Are 'trousers' singular or plural?"

The teacher replied, "They're singular on top and plural on the bottom.

One afternoon at Shrewsbury School, a group of sixth-formers were attending one of their first classes in psychology. The topic was emotional extremes.

"Let's begin by discussing some contrasts," said the tutor. He pointed to a student in the front row, "What is the opposite of joy?"

The student thought about it briefly, then answered "Sadness." The tutor asked another student, "What is the opposite of depression?"

She paused then said, "Elation."

"And you," the tutor said to another student sitting at the back, "What about the opposite of woe?"

The student thought for a moment, then replied, "Um, I believe that would be 'giddy up'."

A woman walked into the kitchen to find her husband stalking around with a fly swatter. "What are you doing?" She demanded.

"Hunting flies," he replied. "Oh. Killed any?" She asked.

"Yep, three males and two females," he replied.
Intrigued, she said, "How can you tell?"

"Three were on a beer can, and two were on the phone." he replied.

Albert, an extremely wealthy 65 year-old, arrives at Patshull Park Country Club with a beautiful 25-year-old blonde on his arm.

His buddies at the club are all aghast. They corner him and ask, "Albert, how did you get the trophy girlfriend?"

"Girlfriend!" exclaims, Albert, "She's my wife!"

His friends are shocked, but continue to ask, "So, how'd you persuade her to marry you?"

Albert replies, "I lied about my age."

His friends respond, "What do you mean? Did you tell her you were only 50?"

Albert smiles and says, "No, I told her I was 81."

In the staff canteen, Jim was always showing Bob photos of his dog and saying how clever it was: doing tricks, playing ball, bringing his newspaper and slippers. One day Jim brought in the album from his daughter's wedding so Bob could look through the photos. Bob decided to tease Jim a little and said, "Hang on, where's your precious dog? I'm surprised he wasn't the Best Man!"

Jim looked at Bob as if he was stupid, "Don't be silly, someone had to take the photos."

For a minute Kidderminster Harriers F.C. were in with a chance – then the game started.

In a school in Telford, a little boy just wasn't getting good marks. One day, his teacher was checking his homework and said, "Lee, once again I'm afraid I can only give you two out of ten."

Little Lee looked up at her and said, "Well, Miss, I don't want to scare you, but…"

He stopped, a worried expression appeared on his face.

"What is it? Tell me, Lee," said his teacher kindly.

"Well," said the boy, "my daddy says if I don't get better marks soon, somebody is going to get a spanking."

A man walks into a bank in Madeley and says to the female assistant at the counter, "I want to open a credit account now!"

To which the lady replied, "I beg your pardon, sir, what did you say?"

"Listen cloth-ears," snapped the man aggressively, "I said I want to open a credit account right now."

"Sir, I'm sorry but we do not tolerate rudeness to staff in this bank!"

The clerk left the window and went over to the bank manager and complained to him about her customer. They both returned and the manager asked, "What seems to be the problem here?"

"There's no problem," the man said, "I just won 50 million in the lottery and I want to open a credit account in this bank right now!"

"I see, sir," the manager said, "and this silly old cow is giving you a hard time?"

When the manager of Worcester City started to tell the team about tactics, half the players thought he was talking about a new kind of peppermint.

A police officer arrived at the scene of a major pile up on the A49.

The officer runs over to the front car and asks the driver, "Are you seriously hurt?"

The driver turns to the officer and says, "How the heck should I know? Do I look like a lawyer?"

What do you get if you cross Kidderminster Harriers with an OXO cube?
A laughing stock.

A farmer was driving along a country road near the picturesque village of Upper Walton with a large load of fertiliser. A little boy, playing in front of his home, saw him and called out, "What do you have on your truck?"

"Fertiliser," the farmer replied.

"What are you going to do with it?" asked the little boy.

"Put it on strawberries," answered the farmer.

"You ought to live here," the little boy advised him. "We put sugar and cream on ours."

An old bloke at the bus stop outside Shrewsbury Royal Hospital is talking to the next person in the queue whilst rubbing his head.

"My wooden leg ain't half giving me some gyp," complained the old boy.

The person in the queue looks at him, wondering why he keeps rubbing his head, and says, "Really? Why?"

The old man retorted, "Cos my missus keeps hitting me over the head with it!"

A policeman stops a man in a car in the middle of Ludlow with a sheep in the front seat.

"What are you doing with that sheep, mon?" He asks. "You should take it to a zoo."

The following week, the same policeman sees the same man again with the sheep in the front seat of the car. Both of them are wearing sunglasses. The policeman pulls him over. "I thought you were going to take that sheep to the zoo?"

The man replies, "I did. We had such a good time we are going to the beach this weekend!"

Sam worked in a telephone marketing company in Wellington. One day he walked into his boss's office and said, "I'll be honest with you, I know the economy isn't great, but I have three companies after me, and, with respect, I would like to ask for a pay rise."

After a few minutes of haggling, his manager finally agreed to a 5% pay rise, and Sam happily got up to leave.

"By the way," asked the boss as Sam went to the door, "Which three companies are after you?"

"The electric company, the water company, and the phone company," Sam replied.

It was a quiet night in Oswestry and a man and his wife were fast asleep, when there was an unexpected knock on the door. The man looked at his alarm clock. It was half past three in the morning. "I'm not getting out of bed at this time," he thought and rolled over.

There was another louder knock.

"Aren't you going to answer that?" asked his wife irritably.

So the man dragged himself out of bed and went downstairs. He opened the door to find a strange man standing outside. It didn't take the homeowner long to realise the man was totally drunk.

"Ow bist, mon?" slurred the stranger. "Can you give me a push?" "No, I'm sorry I most certainly can't. It's half past three in the morning and I was in bed," said the man and he slammed the front door.

He went back up to bed and told his wife what happened. "That wasn't very nice of you," she said. "Remember that night we broke down in the pouring rain on the way to pick the kids up from the babysitter, and you had to knock on that man's door to get us started again? What would have happened if he'd told us to get lost?"

"But the man who just knocked on our door was drunk," replied her husband.

"Well, we can at least help move his car somewhere safe and sort him out a taxi," said his wife. "He needs our help."

So the husband got out of bed again, got dressed, and went downstairs. He opened the door, but couldn't to see the stranger anywhere so he shouted, "Hey, do you still want a push?"

In answer, he heard a voice call out, "Yes please!"

So, still unable to see the stranger, he shouted, "Where are you?"

"I'm over here, mucker," the stranger replied, "on your swing."

The president of the Ludlow Vegetarian Society really couldn't control himself any more. He simply had to try some pork, just to see what it tasted like. So one day he told his members he was going away for a short break. He left town and headed to a restaurant in Shrewsbury. He sat down, ordered a roasted pig, and waited impatiently for his treat. After only a few minutes, he heard someone call his name, and, to his horror, he saw one of his members walking towards him. At exactly the same moment, the waiter arrived at his table, with a huge platter, holding a whole roasted pig with an apple in its mouth. "Isn't this place something?" said the president, thinking quickly, "Look at the way they serve apples!"

Phil's nephew came to him with a problem. "I have my choice of two women," he said, with a worried frown, "A beautiful, penniless young girl whom I love dearly, and a rich widow who I don't really love."

"Follow your heart," Phil counselled, "marry the girl you love."

"Very well, Uncle Phil," said the nephew, "That's sound advice. Thank you."

"You're welcome," replied Phil with a smile, "By the way, where does the widow live?"

Q: What do you call a cat that lives in an igloo?
A: An eskimew!

A farmer from the Worcestershire once visited a farmer based near Whitchurch. The visitor asked, "How big is your farm?" to which the Shropshire farmer replied, "Can you see those trees over there? That's the boundary of my farmland."

"Is that all?" said the Worcestershire farmer, "It takes me three days to drive to the boundary of my farm." The Whitchurch man looked at him and said, "I had a car like that once."

A high-rise building was going up in Telford, and three steel erectors sat on a girder having their lunch.

"Oh, no, not cheese and pickle again," said Jim, the first one, "If I get the same again tomorrow, I'll jump off the girder.'

Horace opened his packet. "Oh, no, not a chicken salad with lettuce and mayo," he said. "If I get the same again tomorrow, I'll jump off too."

Andy, the third man, opened his lunch. "Oh, no, not another potato sandwich," he said. "If I get the same again tomorrow, I'll follow you two off the girder."

The next day, Jim got cheese and pickle. Without delay, he jumped. Horace saw he had chicken salad with lettuce and mayo, and, with a wild cry, he leapt too. Then the third man,

Andy, opened his lunchbox. "Oh, no," he said. "Potato sandwiches." And he too jumped.

The foreman, who had overheard their conversation, reported what had happened, and the funerals were held together.

"If only I'd known," sobbed Jim's wife.

"If only he'd said," wailed Horace's wife.

"I don't understand it at all," said Andy's wife. "He always got his own sandwiches ready."

The nervous young batsman playing for Market Drayton C.C. was having a very bad day. In a quiet moment in the game, he muttered to the one of his team-mates, "Well, I suppose you've seen worse players."

There was no response...so he said it again, "I said 'I guess you've seen worse players.'"

His team-mate looked at him and answered, "I heard you the first time. I was just trying to think..."

Q: Why did the chewing gum cross the road?
A: It was stuck to the chicken's foot.

One day at the Princess Royal Hospital, a group of primary school children were being given a tour. A nurse showed them the x-ray machines and asked them if they had ever had broke a bone.

One little boy raised his hand, "I did!"

"Did it hurt?" the nurse asked.

"No!" he replied.

"Wow, you must be a very brave boy!" said the nurse. "What did you break?"

"My sister's arm!"

A woman from Madeley called Mandy was still not married at thirty-five and she was getting really tired of going to family weddings especially because her old Aunt Maud always came over and said, "You're next!"

It made Mandy so annoyed she racked her brains to figure out how to get Aunt Maud to stop. Sadly, an old uncle died and there was a big family funeral. Mandy spotted Aunt Maud in the crematorium, walked over, pointed at the coffin and said, with a big smile, "You're next!"

At The Royal Fountain Inn in Cleobury Mortimer, a newcomer asked an elderly local regular, "Have you lived here all your life?" The old man took a sip of his ale and, after a long pause, replied, "Dunna know yet!"

One day a Worcestershire boy was in the back garden shouting,

"Mum, why is my Worcester City top lying on the grass?"

His Mum looked out the window and shouted, "The thieving gits stole my pegs!"

At a school in Wellington, the maths teacher poses a question to little Wayne, "If I give £500 to your dad on 12% interest per annum, what will I get back after two years."

"Nowt," says Wayne.

"I am afraid you know nothing about maths, Wayne," says the teacher crossly.

"I am afraid too, sir," replies Wayne, "You dunna know nowt about my father."

A man and his wife walked past a swanky new restaurant in Ludlow. "Did you smell that food?" the woman asked. "Wonderful!"

Being the kind-hearted, generous man that he was, her husband thought, "What the heck, I'll treat her!" So they walked past it a second time.

Peter walked up to the sales lady in the clothing department of large store in Telford.

"I would like to buy my wife a pretty pair of tights," he said. "Something cute with love-hearts or flower patterns."

"Oh, that's so sweet," exclaimed the sales lady, "I'll bet she'll be really surprised." "I'll say," said Peter, "she's expecting a new diamond ring!"

A man from Worcester went into a hardware store and asked to buy a sink. "Would you like one with a plug?" asked the assistant.

"Don't tell me they've gone electric now!" said the man.

Did you hear about the last wish of the henpecked husband of a house-proud wife?

He asked to have his ashes scattered on the carpet.

Have you heard about the latest machine in the arcade in Shrewsbury city centre?

You put ten pence in and ask it any question and it gives you a true answer. One visitor from Worcester tried it last week.

He asked the machine "Where is my father?" The machine replied: "Your father is fishing on the River Stour."

"Well," he thought, "That's daft for a start because my father is dead." Next he asked, "Where is my mother's husband?"

The reply came back, "Your mother's husband is buried in Redditch, but your father is still fishing on the River Stour."

A golfer was going around the Astbury Golf Club course. He was talking to his caddy between holes about a forthcoming competition. "I've been drawn against Jack Smith from Clun, is he any good?"

The caddy checked for a moment and said, "He's absolutely rubbish. Can't get around the course with any ease. He set a new course record for the worst round ever that has only just been beaten."

"Oh, I should easily get through to the next round then, shan't I?" said the golfer complacently.

The caddy looked down at the scorecard and said, "I wouldn't bet on it!"

Three sisters aged 92, 94 and 96 live in a house together in Cleobury Mortimer. One night the 96 year-old draws a bath. She puts her foot in and pauses. She yells to the other sisters, "Were I getting in or out of the bath, love?"

The 94 year-old hollers back, "I dunna know. I'll come up and see." She starts up the stairs but then she pauses, "Were I going upstairs or down, love?"

The 92 year-old is sitting at the kitchen table having tea listening to her sisters. She shakes her head and says, "I hope I never gets that forgetful, knock on wood." She raps on the oak table loudly. Then she shouts upstairs, "I'll come up and help the pair of yer as soon as I see who's at the door."

A Hurrah Henry from Worcester was driving around Telford in his fancy new BMW and realised that he was lost. The driver stopped a local character, old Tom, and said, "Hey, you there! Old man, what happens if I turn left here?"

"Dunna know, sir," replied Tom.

"Well, what if I turn right here - where will that take me?" continued the visitor.

"Dunna know, sir," replied old Tom.

Becoming exasperated, the driver continued, "Well, what if I go straight on?"

A flicker of knowledge passed over old Tom's face but then he replied, "Dunna know, sir."

"I say, old man, you don't know a lot do you?" retorted the posh bloke.

Old Tom looked at him and said, "I may not know a lot, sir, but I ain't lost like what you are!" With that, old Tom walked off leaving the motorist stranded.

Three blondes were walking in the woods near Church Stretton when they came upon a set of tracks.

The first blonde said, "Those are deer tracks."

The second blonde said, "No, those are horse tracks."

The third blonde said, "You're both wrong, those are cattle tracks."

The Blondes were still arguing when the 11.45 train to Cardiff Central hit them.

A labourer in Dawley shouted up to his roofer mate on top of an old terraced house, saying, "Don't start climbing down this ladder, Bert."

"Why not?" Bert called back.

"Cos I moved it five minutes ago!" replied his mate.

A bloke walked up to the foreman of a road laying gang in Shrewsbury and asked for a job. "I haven't got one for you today," said the foreman, looking up from his newspaper. "But if you walk half a mile down there, you'll find the gang and you can see if you like the work. I can put you on the list for tomorrow."

"That's great, mate," said the bloke as he wandered off down the road.

At the end of the shift, the man walked past the foreman and shouted, "Thanks, mate. See you in the morning."

The foreman looked up from his paper and called back, "You've enjoyed yourself then?"

"Yes, I have!" the bloke shouted, "But can I have a shovel or a pick to lean on like the rest of the gang tomorrow?"

A reporter from The Shrewsbury Star was covering the West Midlands football league and went to see Shifnal Town versus Elllesmere Rangers . One of the Shifnal Town players looked so old, he went over to him and said, "You know you might be the oldest man playing in the league. How do you do it at your age?"

The man replied, "I drink six pints of ale every night, smoke two packets of fags a day, and eat loads of bacon cobs."

"Wow, that is incredible!" said the reporter, "How old did you say you were?"

"Twenty-two," said the player proudly.

In Dorrington, two neighbours greet each other over the garden fence.

"Ow bist, mucker? How yer doin'?"

"Poor old grand-dad's died this morning," says the neighbour, "He was out in the garden pulling up cabbages and he went, just like that – we think it was his heart."

"What a shame," commiserates the man next door, "What're you gonna do now?"

"Open a tin of peas," says the neighbour.

An old chap from Ellesmere went to the G.P.

"Doctor," says the old boy, "I am sweating cobs and I feel right under the weather."

"Flu?" asks the doc.

"No," says the old chap, "I rode here on me bike like I always do."

Anne and Matt, a Ludlow couple, went to the Shropshire County Show and found a weighing scale that tells your fortune and weight. "Hey, listen to this," said Matt, showing his wife a small white card. "It says I'm bright, energetic, and a great husband." "Yeah," Anna said, "And it has your weight wrong as well."

A police officer was patrolling the lanes outside Ludlow one night, when he noticed a car swerving all over the road. Quickly, he turned on his lights and siren and pulled the driver over. "Sir, do you know you're all over the road? Please step out of the car."

When the man got out of the car, the policeman told him to walk in a straight line.

"I'd be happy to, offisher," said the drunk, "If you can just get the line to stop moving about."

A bloke from Oswestry goes into an artist's studio and asks if the artist could paint a picture of him surrounded by beautiful, scantily clad women. The artist agrees but he is intrigued by this strange request. He asks his new client why he wants such a picture painted and the bloke says, "Well, if I die before me missus when she finds this painting she'll wonder which one I spent all me money on!"

The next day the bloke's wife goes into the artist's studio and asks him to paint her wearing a big diamond necklace and matching earrings.

"Of course, madam," says the artist, "but may I ask why?"

"Well," replies the woman, "if I die before me husband I want his new woman to be frantic searching for all me jewellery!"